Invasive Species Takeover

ASIAN CARP

BARBARA CILETTI

BLACK
RABBIT
BOOKS

BOLT

Bolt is published by Black Rabbit Books
P.O. Box 3263, Mankato, Minnesota, 56002.
www.blackrabbitbooks.com
Copyright © 2017 Black Rabbit Books

Design and Production by Michael Sellner
Photo Research by Rhonda Milbrett

Library of Congress Control Number: 2015954686

HC ISBN: 978-1-68072-013-6   PB ISBN: 978-1-68072-277-2

Printed in the United States at CG Book Printers,
North Mankato, Minnesota, 56003. PO #1793 4/16

Web addresses included in this book were working and appropriate
at the time of publication. The publisher is not responsible for broken
or changed links.

Image Credits
Alamy: Carlyn Iverson/Stocktrek
Images, 8–9, 28 (right); Corbis: Wil
Meinderts/Buiten-beeld/Minden Pictures,
13 (inset), 27; Flickr: Dan O'Keefe, Michigan
Sea Grant, 31; Kate Gardiner, 10; Sam Stukel, 6, 28
(left); Getty: ullstein bild, 20; iagreatlakes.com: 24;
invadingspecies.com: 22 (all); jasonlindsey.com: Jason
Lindsey, 4–5; Milwaukee Journal Sentinel, reproduced
with permission: 23; Newscom: Gerard LACZ/NHPA/Pho-
toshot, 3; Nancy Stone/MCT, Back Cover, 1, 19 (top); Wil
Meinderts/Buiten-beeld/Min/Newscom, Cover; Purdue
University Department of Forestry and Natural Resources:
Reuben Goforth, 14; Shutterstock: Ivan Mateev, 24–25,
29; leungchopan, 13 (back); Wikimedia: Engbretson,
Eric, 32
Every effort has been made to contact copyright
holders for material reproduced in this book.
Any omissions will be rectified in subse-
quent printings if notice is given
to the publisher.

Contents

CHAPTER 1

Attacked by

The **kayaker** sliced his way through the water. He was trying to win the Missouri River canoe and kayak race. Suddenly, something jumped out of the water. It was a fish. And it was coming toward him. He didn't have time to move. The fish smashed into his head.

The Flying Fish

The fish was an Asian carp. It weighed 30 pounds (14 kilograms). The fish gave the man a pounding headache. He couldn't finish the race.

Asian carp are known for their jumping. Some people call them flying fish. The fish jump when surprised by boats.

NOSTRILS

EYE

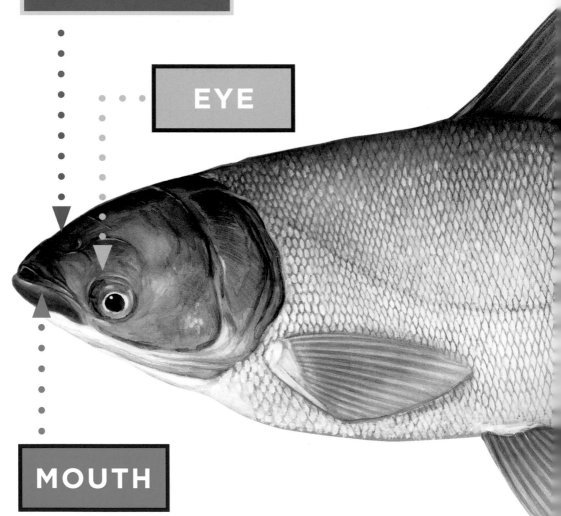

MOUTH

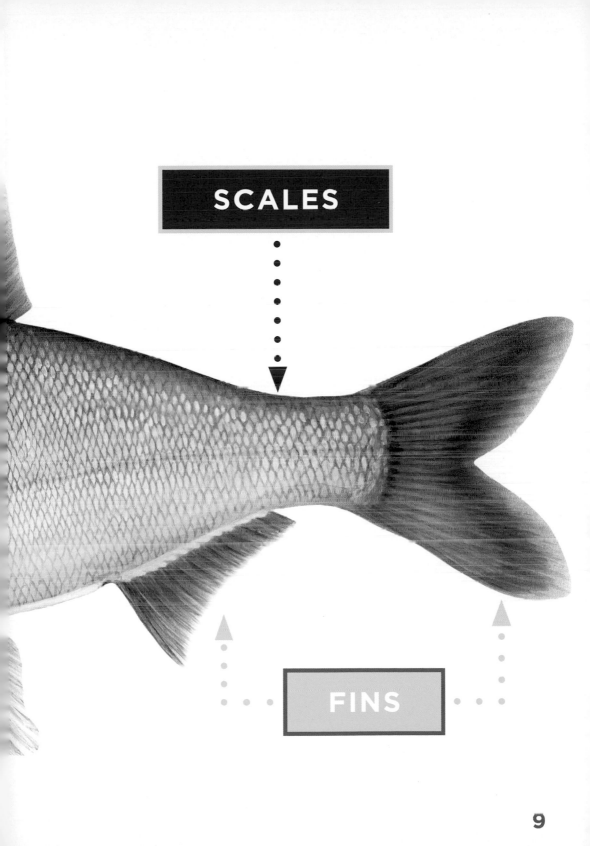

SCALES

FINS

Invasive Species

Asian carp are not supposed to be in the Missouri River. People brought the fish to the United States. The carp quickly spread to new areas. They hurt the animals and plants that already lived there. Asian carp are an **invasive species**.

These fish are not in the Great Lakes yet. But they are getting close. Scientists are worried.

CHAPTER 2

Spreading Out

Asian carp are from southeast Asia. They eat a lot of freshwater plants. That eating keeps the water clean.

In the 1970s, people brought Asian carp to the United States. They planned to control where the carp lived. But floods carried the carp away. The fish washed into rivers.

People used the carp to clean water in fish farms.

14

On the Move

The Asian carp began laying eggs in their new homes. Females can lay 500,000 eggs at a time! The baby fish grow fast. These new carp quickly spread to other water areas. No underwater **predators** are big enough to eat Asian carp. So the **population** continues to grow.

THE SPREAD OF ASIAN CARP

Great Lakes

Canada

CHAPTER 3

Taking Over

Asian carp cause a lot of trouble.
In some streams, they act like bullies.
They force animals that already lived
there to move away.

LIFE CYCLE of an Asian Carp

egg

larval fish

fry

juvenile

adult

Eating Machines

Asian carp eat all the time. Each fish eats up to 40 percent of its body weight every day. They eat the **plankton** that other animals need. Other fish starve to death.

Some carp eat plants along the **shore**. This eating destroys an area's shore.

Some Asian carp eat snails and mussels.

Boat Jumpers

Asian carp can be harmful to people too. The noise from boats scares the fish. The carp leap out of the water. These heavy fish can injure boaters. They also damage boating equipment.

TYPES OF ASIAN CARP
(maximum sizes)

INCHES 0 10

Bighead Carp 60 INCHES (152 cm) **110 POUNDS (50 kg)**

Silver Carp 39 INCHES (99 cm) **60 POUNDS (27 kg)**

Grass Carp 59 INCHES (150 cm) **99 POUNDS (45 kg)**

Black Carp 48 INCHES (122 cm) **71 POUNDS (32 kg)**

POUNDS 0 10

CHAPTER 4

Too Many

Asian carp have spread throughout the Midwest. Scientists are working to stop the spread. They have put up **barriers** to block the fish. But the carp can jump over them.

Stopping the Invasion

Asian carp do a bit of good. They help keep lakes and rivers clean. But without care, these fish take over. That's why these invaders must be stopped.

ASIAN CARP BY THE NUMBERS

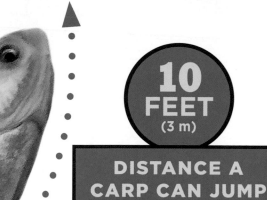

2 TO 4 FEET
(.6 TO 1.2 meters)
AVERAGE LENGTH

10 FEET
(3 m)

DISTANCE A CARP CAN JUMP OUT OF WATER

$18 MILLION

possible cost to keep Asian carp out of the Great Lakes

30 TO 40 POUNDS
(14 to 18 kilograms)

AVERAGE WEIGHT

Think
about It. . .

1. People brought Asian carp to the United States. Should people be allowed to bring animals to other countries? Explain why or why not.

2. Some chemicals could stop Asian carp. Use other sources to find out what effects chemicals could have.

3. Compare common carp with Asian carp. How are they similar? How are they different?

GLOSSARY

barrier (BAR-ee-uhr)—something, such as a fence, that blocks movement from one place to another

invasive species (in-VAY-siv SPEE-seez)—animals or plants that spread through an area where they are not native, often causing problems for native plants and animals

kayaker (KI-ak-uhr)—a person who uses a kayak; a kayak is a long narrow boat that is moved by a paddle with two blades.

plankton (PLANK-tun)—the very small animal and plant life in an ocean, lake, or river

population (pop-yu-LAY-shun)—the whole number of people or animals living in an area

predator (PRED-uh-tuhr)—an animal that eats other animals

shore (SHOR)—the land bordering a body of water

LEARN MORE

Kallio, Jamie. *12 Things to Know about Invasive Species.*
Today's News. Mankato, MN: Peterson Pub. Co., 2015.

O'Connor, Karen. *The Threat of Invasive Species.*
Animal 911: Environmental Threats. New York: Gareth
Stevens Publishing, 2014.

Spilsbury, Richard. *Invasive Species Underwater.*
Invaders from Earth. New York: PowerKids Press, 2015.

WEBSITES

Asian Carp
www.fws.gov/midwest/fisheries/library/fact-asiancarp.pdf

Asian Carp Threat to the Great Lakes
www.nwf.org/Wildlife/Threats-to-Wildlife/Invasive-Species/Asian-Carp.aspx

Silent Invaders
www.youtube.com/watch?v=rPeg1tbBt0A

INDEX